Responsible Pet Care

Pigeons

Responsible Pet Care

Pigeons

CARLIENNE FRISCH

Rourke Publications, Inc.
Vero Beach, FL 32964

Library of Congress Cataloging-in-Publication Data

Frisch, Carlienne, 1944–
     Pigeons / by Carlienne A. Frisch
          p. cm. – (Responsible pet care)
     Includes bibliographical references.
     Summary: Discusses the varieties, housing, feeding,
handling, training, showing, and breeding of pigeons.
     ISBN 0-86625-193-6
     1. Pigeons–Juvenile literature. [1. Pigeons.] I. Title.
II. Series: Responsible pet care (Vero Beach, Fla.)
SF465.F75 1991
636.5'96–dc20   90-25412
                                                                      CIP
                                                                       AC

CONTENTS

Is A Pigeon For You?

Keeping pigeons is fun, whether you want the companionship of a tame bird, the pleasure of competing in shows and exhibitions, or the excitement of racing the birds. Pigeons are easily tamed and pleasant to have around. Their voices are soft, and they have little odor. They have definite, individual personalities. They usually are good parents.

A pigeon's purchase price is reasonable and food costs are low. The birds can live in a variety of conditions, whether in a city apartment or a country **loft**.

Pigeons have been close to people for centuries. They were food for Egyptians and messengers for the ancient Chinese and the early Greeks. Ancient Hebrews used pigeons as religious sacrifices. The dove, another term for pigeon, is the most-mentioned bird in the Bible. It symbolizes purity and the Holy Spirit. The dove also is sacred in Muslim countries.

The wild pigeon, or barn pigeon, is commonly seen in cities.

These homing pigeons are returning to their loft after a long flight. No one knows exactly how they find their way home.

Commanders of ancient armies used pigeons as messengers in place of people on foot or horseback. In World War II, the British and Americans used pigeons for the same purpose. Some people believe that early aviators learned trick maneuvers, such as loops, from watching the flight of pigeons.

Today, pigeons are used for laboratory research, exhibiting, racing and homing, sending messages, and for their meat. The commercial market for **squab**, or young pigeon meat, is small, however. About 90 percent of pigeons raised in the United States are for exhibition, hobby, or pleasure.

There are about 300 pigeon varieties. Some have strong endurance and homing instincts, while others have fancy colors. Before you choose the kind of pigeon to get, you must decide on your aim as a pigeon owner.

7

Varieties of Pigeons

All of the domestic breeds of pigeons are believed to have descended from the Blue Rock Dove, which lives in Europe, Asia, and Africa. The first domestic pigeons were probably brought to America by colonists.

People have bred pigeons for various purposes. Pleasure breeds include those that are flyers and those that look fancy. Flying pigeons, which perform in exhibitions, include rollers, tipplers, skycutters, and tumblers. Tumblers do loops and somersaults—in the air or on the ground. They are the acrobats of pigeon breeds!

Show pigeons include fantails, jacobins, modenas, carriers, pouters, owls, and trumpeters. The fantail, which may have originated in India, struts along with its head bent far back to show off its broad, fancy "peacock" tail. The jacobin has a large feather hood that nearly hides its head. When the pouter inflates its neck into a large globe, it looks like a man of bygone days in formal clothing, tight-fitting breeches, and, perhaps, a full beard.

Fantail pigeons like to show off their fancy tails. They are often seen at exhibitions.

The Blue Rock Dove is the ancestor of all domestic pigeon breeds.

The carrier pigeon is often confused with the racing homer. The carrier, however, is a fancy show breed. It has beak **wattles**, and rough-textured skin, called **cere**, around its eyes. The owl breed of pigeon, which is no relation to an actual owl, may have such a short beak that it is unable to feed its young.

Racing homers, or homing pigeons, have a strong drive to return to the loft or nest. They may have a special sense or they may be guided by the earth's magnetic field. Perhaps they use the sun as a compass, even on a cloudy day. Most people believe the birds follow familiar landmarks. Racing pigeons are bred and trained with great care, like race horses.

Utility pigeons are bred to have heavy breasts for eating. They include the white king, hungarian, maltese, mondain, Carneau, and giant homer.

The runt, which is the largest and oldest pigeon breed, is used in cross-breeding to increase the weight of other breeds. It is not used for show or for food.

9

Choosing Your Pigeons

After you decide whether you want flying pigeons, show pigeons, racing homers, or meat birds, you'll need advice on which breeds you might get. You can read the *American Pigeon Journal* or the *Encyclopedia of Pigeon Breeds*. You can also consult the National Pigeon Association in Riverton, Utah, and the American Dove Association in Milton, Kentucky, for the names of reliable breeders.

If you don't want to keep your pigeons confined, get young birds. Older birds must be kept locked up to keep them from returning to their previous homes.

Never purchase culls, or below-average birds. For cage-kept birds, it is best to get a mated pair from a reliable breeder. A pair is not simply one of each sex. It is one of each sex that already have mated and usually are leg-banded. If you buy pigeons from more than one breeder, and not in pairs, make sure the types will be compatible for mating.

Rollers are easy to maintain, and are a good choice for a beginning pigeon fancier.

10

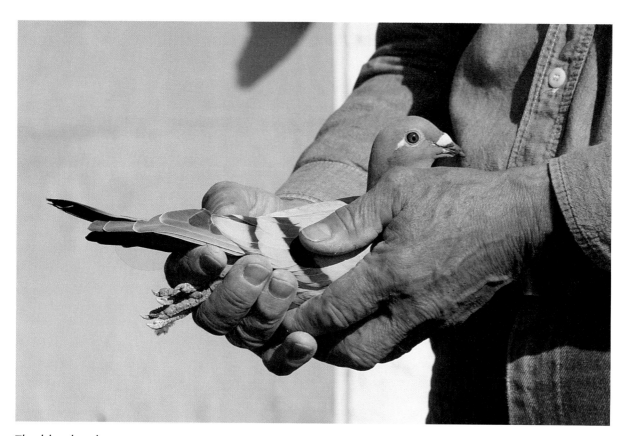

The blue bar homing pigeon has striped wings.

It is difficult to tell the sex of pigeons before they are old enough to mate. The male, or **cock**, usually is more aggressive. He coos, struts, and fans his tail to the ground. The female, or **hen**, waddles. When she puts her beak into the cock's mouth, he feeds her small amounts of feed from his **crop**. This is called "billing and cooing." Two birds acting this way are a pair and should be kept together.

Look for healthy birds with clear eyes, good balance, easy breathing, and no signs of loose droppings. Do not get birds from a dealer who has canker, or trichomoniasis, in the **flock**.

The best breeds for a novice pigeon **fancier** are Chinese owls, English trumpeters, fantails, Indian fantails, helmets, lahores, modenas, rollers, and tipplers. The diamond dove from Australia makes a good house pet if you have an extra-large cage.

Wild doves or wild pigeons cannot be kept well in a bird cage. They need an **aviary**.

Understanding Pigeons

Pigeons are social birds. They enjoy one another's company. They like to live in groups, or flocks. They communicate through a variety of sounds. In city parks, if one pigeon finds food, it is soon joined by other pigeons.

Pigeons have keen eyesight and hearing, color vision, and, unlike most birds, a sense of smell. They also have an excellent sense of where their home is. They will always return home after flying loose unless caught by a **predator**, such as a hawk, or meeting with an accident.

Pigeons have rounded heads, plump bodies, short legs, and short beaks. They walk well on land and are experts in the air.

Pigeons enjoy being around other pigeons. They communicate through a variety of sounds.

The flight feathers are strong and light. They help the pigeon fly.

The pigeon's body is covered with dense, sleek feathers that keep the bird cool in hot weather and warm in the winter. The flight and tail feathers are light, tough, and flexible. They help the pigeon to fly. The contour feathers give the bird its pretty, smooth look and protect it from extreme temperatures. Under the contour feathers are downy feathers. They are fluffy and also provide insulation. In the Chinese owl pigeon, some of the contour feathers make a **frill**, and downy feathers decorate the bird's legs.

When the pigeon **preens** itself, it pulls each feather through its beak. It oils its feathers with its beak to make them waterproof. The oil comes from a gland at the base of the tail.

Each year, pigeons molt, or lose their old feathers and replace them with new ones. The molt is gradual, lasting about six months.

Pigeons eat often and digest quickly. Because the bird has no teeth with which to chew, it must swallow grit to help digest the food in its **gizzard**, or stomach.

Most birds tilt their heads back to swallow water, but pigeons do not. They drink by sucking up water, as if they were using a straw. They learn how to eat and drink from their parents.

Housing

The pigeon house is called a loft or cote. The typical loft consists of a building for shelter and an attached flight space, or aviary. Provide at least four square feet in the building and the same amount of space in the flight enclosure for each pair. A sanded floor makes it easy to keep the loft clean with monthly raking. You can build nest boxes in a series on the back wall, from two feet above the floor to eye level.

Build the loft so it faces south, especially in a cold climate. A loft can be built in the tip of a barn or as a separate building on the ground. In some cities, you may build a pigeon loft on the roof of your house.

A cote, or loft, is a small house made especially for pigeons. The attached aviary is covered with wire mesh.

These pigeons feel right at home inside their loft. The owner built nesting boxes for 30 pigeons.

For the aviary, use wire with holes no larger than one inch to keep out sparrows, rats, and other disease-carriers. Make the pen the same width as the loft, but no higher than seven feet. At each end, put a landing platform at a four-foot height, six inches from the wire. Use cedar or redwood that is 8–12 inches wide and at least one inch thick.

You may keep a pair of pigeons in a three-foot-square box with a wire front. Cages can be hung from the ceiling with heavy wire that keeps the cage from swaying. Install two nesting boxes on the back wall of the cage.

The pigeon equipment you'll need includes waterers, feeders, a grit hopper, perches, and a lock on the loft to prevent pigeon theft. Birds in a loft also need a shallow bath pan that is filled with water. It should be refilled whenever it starts to get dirty.

Feeding And Watering

Pigeons rarely have nutritional problems, but cleanliness in feeding and watering is necessary to prevent disease. Clean the waterers daily and feeders at least once a week.

It is easy to make sturdy, inexpensive feeders and waterers. Cut out part of one side of a clean plastic jug, either half-gallon or gallon. Leave enough bottom lip on the cut side to fill with feed and water. Pigeons need at least three-fourths of an inch of water at all times.

In purchasing feed, figure 100 pounds of grain per pair per year. You can buy pigeon grain already mixed, or you can prepare your own. Make a mix of 30 percent cracked corn, 20 percent kafir, 20 percent red wheat, 25 percent Canadian peas, and a 5-percent mix of barley, hulled oats, and rice. Once a week, add small amounts of hemp or millet seed. You can also add chicken layer pellets to the mix.

Pigeon feed is made up of many grains, such as corn, kafir, peas, and millet seed.

In addition to a feeder and waterer, a pigeon loft should include a grit hopper. Pigeons and other birds need grit to help them digest their food.

If you mix the feed, buy mechanically dried grains rather than field-dried, which may become moldy. Never feed damp, mildewed, dirty, discolored, or vermin-contaminated feed. Spoiled feed can cause diarrhea and death.

Pigeons also need grit and salt. Ground pigeon mineral (health grit) contains both. You'll need about five pounds per year, per pair. In addition, pigeons need a small amount of crushed oyster shell for good egg shell formation.

Pigeons tend to overeat and overfeed their young, so the fancier must exercise some control. Fanciers with only a few pairs usually set the food out twice a day. Those with a larger flock that is fed "cafeteria style," with ingredients in separate, adjacent containers, put covers over the food at the end of each feeding time.

Handling and Banding

Many pigeons are tame enough to be picked up, especially those kept in a cage and trained for exhibitions. If you have difficulty catching a pigeon, you can use a fish net.

To hold a pigeon, grasp the bird so your thumb is clasped over the pigeon's back and your fingers make a circle around the breast. The legs should be securely held between your fingers. This keeps the wings close to the bird's body and prevents injury to the bird or its feathers.

Banding is an important part of keeping pigeons. In some communities, a banded bird is protected by law from human harm. Banding helps the pigeon fancier keep flock records and is necessary for any bird that will be exhibited. Bands also help in recovering lost or stolen pigeons.

A pigeon's identification number is printed on its leg band. This helps the owner keep track of the bird and maintain accurate records.

When handling a pigeon, be sure to keep the wings close to the bird's body. The bird pictured above is a white grizzle homing pigeon.

A numbered band is like the pigeon's social security number or military serial number. The band, which remains on the bird for life, has the year it was banded and the bird's individual identification number. The fancier records the number in the flock's permanent records.

To band a week-old squab, or young pigeon, slip a numbered metal ring on its leg by pressing together the three front toes and sliding the band over them and up over the fourth toe. It is best to have another person holding the pigeon securely.

When a pair mates, many pigeon fanciers slip a plastic band on one leg of each pigeon, using a different color for each pair. The plastic bands can be obtained with pairs of duplicate numbers to make record-keeping easy.

Training

Pigeons may be trained for homing or for showing in exhibitions. By instinct, a young homer will return to its loft from a distance of 5 to 10 miles. You can use this instinct to train a pigeon to come home from longer distances. Some birds have raced home from 50 miles away.

First, put the bird on the landing platform outside the loft. It will fly around outside of the loft, but you can coax it back inside with food. When it is familiar with that area, take the bird in a covered basket about half a mile from the loft and turn it loose. Try to return home before it does, or have someone else there to encourage the bird to go into the loft and eat.

Lofts made for homing pigeons should include small landing platforms. The lofts don't need aviaries, beause the birds naturally return home if turned loose.

A pigeon fancier releases his homing pigeons from a special cage.

Continue this practice often, increasing the distance by about one mile each time. Various pigeon clubs sponsor races of short distances for young birds and longer flights for seasoned "pilots" (older birds).

To train a pigeon for exhibitions, use a show stick. This is a one-fourth- inch dowel stick, 15–18 inches long, with rounded ends. Put the pigeon in a cage. If the bird needs to stand more erect, touch it gently under the breast with the stick. If it carries its tail down, tap the bird at the base of the tail. If a fantail does not tilt back enough, touch it near the crop or the upper part of the breast.

A bird that is trained to display itself will go into a show stance whenever someone approaches the cage. The bird is then ready to enter a pigeon show.

Showing

It is easy to tell a blue-and-black racing pigeon from a show bird. A show bird may look quite unusual, such as the pouter with the inflated throat, the jacobin with a cowl of feathers, or the fantail, which stands on tiptoe and bends its head back to touch its peacock-like tail.

Birds are entered in shows according to breed, variety, and sex. Training and grooming for a show are very important. The bird must be in good health, with a perfectly balanced and proportioned body, and able to show excellent feathers. Never show a bird in molt.

Before a show, clip the bird's beak with nail clippers so the upper and lower parts of the beak are the same length. Do not clip too far back. Cut or trim any toenails that have grown too long or are crooked. Pluck abnormally shaped or colored feathers from the feet, legs, or other parts of the body.

A pigeon's toenails may need to be trimmed before a show. Be careful!

A bird to be shown must be well-proportioned and in excellent health, like this white grizzle.

To speed up new feather growth during molting, give feeds of higher protein content, such as Canadian peas or field peas.

Do not bathe the pigeon for three or four days before the show. This allows a glossy sheen to build up naturally. Put sawdust on the floor of the loft to keep the bird clean during this time. To clean tail or wing feathers soiled by droppings, soap the feathers with a shaving brush, working a lather of pure soap and water into the soiled area. Rinse with lukewarm water, dry with paper towels, and put the bird in a basket or cage in a warm spot until it dries.

Dust the bird with special insecticide powder the day before the show, put it into a show basket, and leave it there overnight. Do not put more than one pigeon in each section of the basket. At the show, smooth or bend ruffled feathers into shape if possible. This is called shaping. You may also need to wash a soiled feather or two just before the show begins.

Breeding

Pigeons mate for life and will remain true to each other unless separated by time, distance, or death. Never leave an unmated pigeon with a pair. It will cause trouble by trying to steal a mate.

When a pair have gone through the billing and cooing described in the third chapter, they are ready to build a nest. Each pair will need two nesting boxes, because they will continue to raise their young in the first nest while laying and setting on eggs in the second nest.

Nest boxes can be as simple as two wooden boxes about 12 inches square, attached to a wall. With a good supply of nesting materials, such as soft pine needles, clean hay, or tobacco stems (which may be bought at a pigeon supply store), the pair will work together to build a nest. The nest will look untidy and flimsy, but it will be perfect for the two eggs the hen will lay a day apart.

This is a mated pair of blue bar homers. Pigeons mate for life.

A nesting box can be very simple. Be sure to provide a generous amount of nesting material, such as the hay shown above.

The cock will set on the eggs from morning until late afternoon. Then the hen will take her turn. In 16 or 17 days, the first egg will hatch. The other egg, which was laid a day later, will hatch the next day. Some hens lay only one egg, while a few lay three. If three eggs are laid, they will hatch over three days. A few days after the eggs hatch, the hen will go to the other nest and lay another two eggs. She and the cock will take turns setting on the eggs and feeding the young in the first nest.

Pigeons will exhaust themselves if permitted to raise young year-round. You should separate the hens and cocks when molting season begins, in early August, and not permit them to begin breeding again for six months. When you separate the pair, clean the nest boxes and burn old nesting material.

The Young

When squabs hatch, they are very tiny, weak, and helpless. They cannot walk or even hold their heads up. Their eyes are shut and their bodies are wet. They will be hungry in a few hours, however, and then they will begin to grow.

The parents carry the empty shells out of the nest and drop them on the ground nearby. When the babies are ready, both parents feed them "pigeon milk." It is a white, cheesy substance created in the parents' crops just for feeding newly hatched squabs. The parents force the pigeon milk down the throats of the squabs. The babies grow quickly on this high-protein food, doubling in weight in two days. After a week, the parents add partly digested grain to the milk. Soon, they are feeding only grain. Sometimes the squab that is one day older will eat more and grow more quickly.

A blue check homing pigeon sets on its eggs. In this case the owner had to provide only nesting material, as the nesting boxes are built into the loft wall.

At the age of one week, these archangel squabs are small and helpless.

After a week, the squab's eyes will open. **Pin feathers** will appear, along with some **plumage** color. At 10 days, the young will hiss and snap harmlessly at people. By the time they are three weeks old, the young birds sit or stand around the nest area. If disturbed, they puff themselves up, open their bills wide, and snap them shut with a loud popping sound. They flap their wings and try to hit an observer that gets too close.

At four to six weeks, the squabs have reached their peak of growth and are ready to leave the nest. The parents want to be rid of them. The squabs are ready for the commercial meat market, for sale to another fancier, or to be kept for breeding.

If the parents should die and you are left with orphan squabs, try to put them with a pair that will take care of them. If, however, you must hand-feed the young, use an eyedropper or syringe. Mash pigeon pellets and add boiling water to make a soup-like liquid. Let the mixture cool. Feed the birds at least three times daily. After a week, use less water and reduce feeding times to twice daily. You may use baby formula or evaporated milk in place of water.

Health and Ailments

Healthy pigeons live for 10 to 15 years. The most common diseases that affect pigeons are trichomoniasis, pigeon pox, and colds. Mites and lice also can cause problems. A sick pigeon may have loose droppings, weight loss, a tilted head, difficulty in balancing, or swollen joints. You can treat many problems at home after getting the help of a veterinarian in diagnosing what is wrong.

Trichomoniasis, also called trich, is a parasite that causes the disease called canker. The bird will have cheesy material or hard masses in the mouth or throat. It will be weak, suffering from a loss of appetite, loose droppings, and shortness of breath. Adult pigeons may carry the disease without being seriously affected, but squabs die from it. It is treated by applying a mild astringent to the throat and by giving the medication Enhaptin in feed, water, or individual capsules.

An owl decoy frightens away predatory birds, such as hawks.

Healthy pigeons live for up to 15 years. These are Swabian, or pheasant, pigeons.

Pigeon pox can be prevented by vaccinating the birds. Because it spreads slowly, a flock can be saved even though one or two birds may already have pox. Symptoms include crusty sores around the bird's mouth or eyes. It can result in sudden death.

A pigeon with a cold may have watery or puffy eyes and make a raspy, rattling sound when it breathes. Some birds may seem normal except they will be warmer than usual when held in the hand. To cure the cold, use antibiotics in the feed or water, or inject them directly into the birds.

Pigeon lice can be controlled by application of a poultry louse powder to each pigeon. Red mites, which live in pigeon buildings, can be eliminated by spraying the premises with malathion. The black or northern fowl mite lives on the bird's body. Use individual application of malathion dust to each bird as a control. You should be aware that malathion can be dangerous— it must be used very carefully. You might want to consult your veterinarian about other chemicals that could be used.

GLOSSARY

Aviary	A large cage covered with metal mesh.
Cere	A rough-textured, waxy skin on the top of a bird's beak, near its eyes.
Cock	A male bird.
Crop	A pouch-like part of a bird's throat in which food is held and softened.
Fancier	A person who has a special interest in an animal, bird, or plant.
Flock	A number of animals or birds kept together.
Frill	A ruff of fur or feathers on an animal's neck.
Gizzard	The muscular part of a bird's stomach, where the food is crushed.
Hen	A female bird.
Loft	A pigeon house, sometimes called a cote.
Pin feathers	Undeveloped feathers that have just come through the skin.
Plumage	The feathers of a bird.
Predator	An animal or bird that hunts and kills other animals or birds for food.
Preen	To clean and smooth the feathers with the bill.
Squab	Young pigeons.
Wattles	A fleshy growth around the beak of a bird.

INDEX

Photographs by Mark E. Ahlstrom

*We would like to thank the following people
for their help in making this book:*

Art Lindberg
Alan Tilson

Produced by Mark E. Ahlstrom
(The Bookworks)
St. Peter, MN

Typesetting and Keylining: The Final Word
Photo Research: Judith A. Ahlstrom